Benjamin Bull

Lessons from the Farm

Carl Saunders, Jr.

Illustrations by Blueberry Illustrations

This book is dedicated to my wife, Heather,
and three children, Jeanna, Trey and Brent.
Thank you for your unwavering love and
support in all of my life adventures!

Benjamin was a big, solid Black Angus bull. Long and muscular from head to toe, he weighed almost 2,000 pounds at only two years old.

He was purchased by a farmer to be one day the father to many other big calves. The farmer wanted the best bull his money could buy. Benjamin was the best around.

Benjamin was a quiet, peaceful bull. He mostly enjoyed laying in the shade of the large oak tree, which grew perfectly in the middle of the pasture. From there, Benjamin could see in all directions.

Life on the farm was hard work. Day after day the farmer, like farmers do, put on his boots and went out to the barn. No matter how hot or cold, no matter if it was raining or snowing, no matter if the wind blew or the sky was still, he fed the cattle.

Every day, upon getting a glimpse of the farmer, the cows, the calves, and Benjamin would make their way over to enjoy their meal.

Benjamin was by far the biggest animal in the pasture. He could easily have pushed the smaller cattle out of his way so that he could be first to eat the best of the hay bales or the finest of the grains, but he didn't.

One summer day, the farmer and his young son spent the afternoon at the livestock auction, where farmers would come from all around to buy or sell their animals. The auction was an exciting place, always bustling with animals making their animal noises, people talking to one another, and, above all, the auctioneer calling.

That particular day, the farmer's son saw a cute, but small and skinny, black and white Holstein calf. He was puny and frail and the farmer didn't even know whether he would survive the winter, unless a farmer, like farmers do, took special care to make sure he was warm and fed.

When the farmer raised his hand to bid for the calf, he could see the excitement in his son's eyes and the smile that spread across the young boy's face when the auctioneer shouted "Sold," and the little calf was theirs!

The little calf didn't fit in with all those big Angus cattle. When he stood beside big Benjamin, "Dots," as the young boy called him, looked the size of an apple standing next to a watermelon.
He was barely old enough to be away from his Mama when he was taken to the auction.

He could be seen wandering around the pasture, mooing and trying to find a mother to call his own, but the other cows didn't want a new calf in their group, much less a puny Holstein. Dots was an outsider.

And so it continued. The summer months turned into autumn months and day after day, the farmer, like farmers do, brought hay and grain to the cattle, who came running to the sound of the grain hitting the feed trough.

Although Dots came running for food, he was usually pushed aside and rarely got much grain, if any at all. He was all alone, or so he thought.

Then one unusual day, as the farmer was dumping grain into the trough, he noticed that Benjamin hadn't come to eat. Curious, the farmer looked across the pasture.

Far from the shade of his oak tree, Benjamin was standing by an old maple tree, where many branches had fallen and the once deep roots were now exposed.

While all the other cattle were loudly enjoying their meal, acting as if nothing were out of the ordinary, there was Benjamin, not running or even walking toward the food.

The farmer worried that something must be wrong with Benjamin, as he always came to eat. He was, after all, the biggest animal in the field. So after emptying the buckets of grain, the farmer, like farmers do, set out to go check on his bull.

The sun was partially setting as
the farmer made the hike to
where Benjamin was standing.

Benjamin was mooing louder and louder the closer the farmer came, continuing to moo as he stood beside him. The farmer carefully examined the bull, but everything looked just fine. But certainly something was wrong!

Then, in those quiet moments as the farmer stood there considering the possibilities, he heard deep sighs and labored breaths. As he began looking around, there on the ground, tangled and stuck between the fallen branches and exposed roots, was Dots.

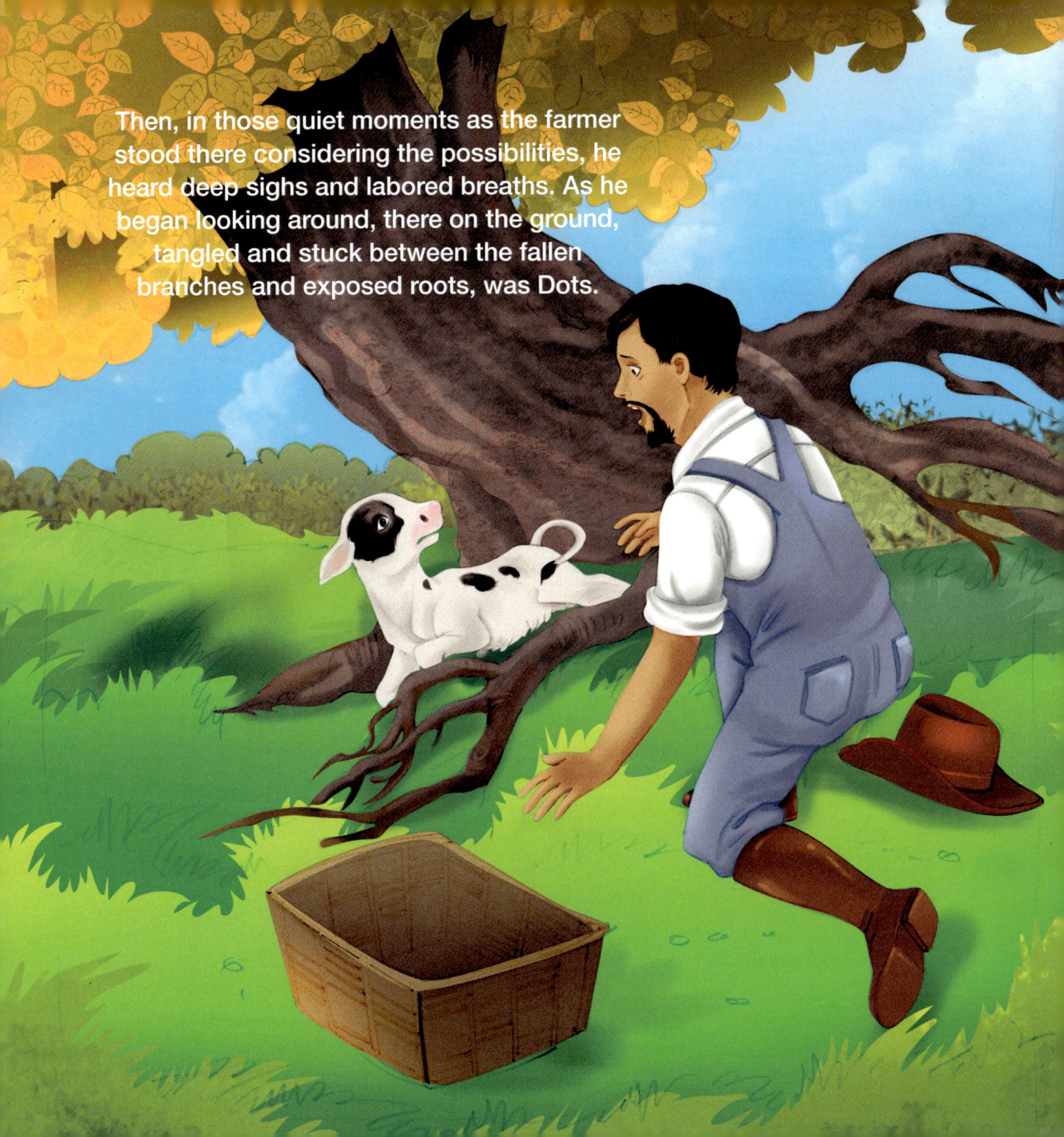

The farmer moved the branches
and untangled the roots that had
wrapped around the little calf.

He helped Dots to his feet and watched the frightened young calf stumble away just as the sun was setting behind the mountains. Out of the corner of his eye, he could see Benjamin slowly heading down the hill toward the empty feed trough.

Walking across the field toward his truck, the farmer thought about how he hadn't noticed that Dots was missing and that none of the other cattle had seemed to care.

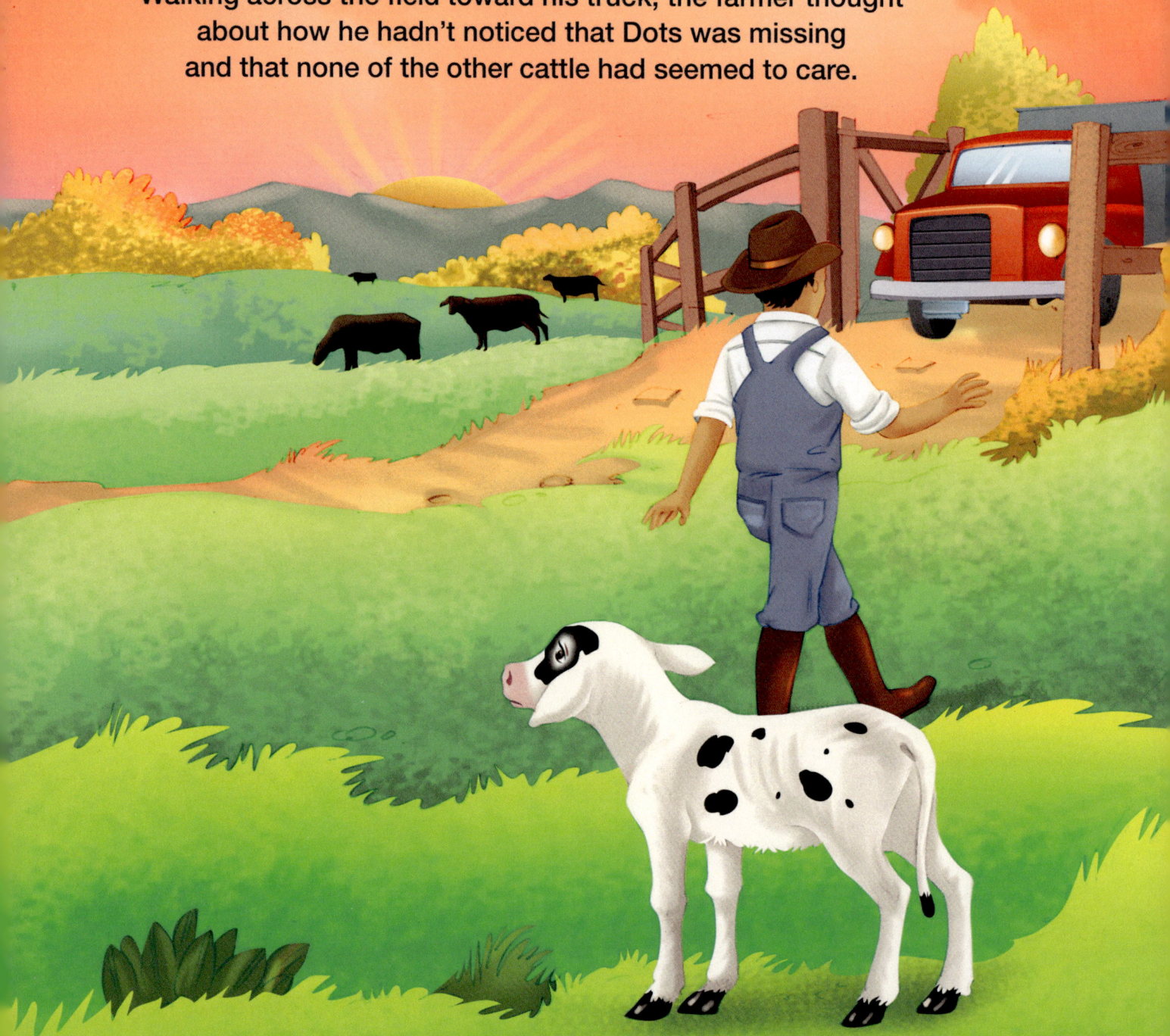

But it was that big bull, a prized bull, the best and most valuable of all the cattle in the field, which took notice. It was Benjamin who had stood at the old maple tree, where even with the smell of grain in the air, he never left the helpless calf.

If it were not for Benjamin standing guard and giving up his portion of grain, the farmer would have missed the chance to untangle Dots and save his life.

As the farmer drove away, he felt fortunate to have a guardian looking out over his field. The farmer made a quiet commitment to be just like Benjamin Bull—strong, but peaceful and caring, and most of all, guarding those in need, no matter how big or small, no matter how valuable or invaluable they may seem.

Because that's what farmers do.

Carl Saunders Jr. is a man of many different roles. He is a board-licensed nurse practitioner and is the director of organ transplantation for LifeNet Health in Virginia. He serves additionally as a supporting partner and medical provider with an international organization that provides medical care and education to some of the poorest areas of the world. Carl's mission in life is to assist others by using the talents with which he has been blessed.

His family owns and operates four livestock farms across the Commonwealth of Virginia. The farming legacy goes back several generations.

He is the proud parent of three beautiful and talented children, and has been married to his beautiful and caring wife for over 17 years.

Made in the USA
Columbia, SC
05 November 2018